500 Ways to Get More Out of Life

500 Ways to Get More Out of Life

Pamela Gillingham

Writers Club Press
San Jose New York Lincoln Shanghai

500 Ways to Get More Out of Life

Writers Club Press
an imprint of iUniverse.com, Inc.

For information address:
iUniverse.com, Inc.
620 North 48th Street, Suite 201
Lincoln, NE 68504-3467
www.iuniverse.com

ISBN: 0-595-13594-3

Printed in the United States of America

Dedication

For Alexander, whose love means the world to me. For Benny who has been by my side through good times as well as bad times. And especially for Stephen whose confidence in me over the years has meant so much.

Epigraph

Life really is what we make of it.

---∞---

Foreword

If we could hear more songs and fewer cries life would sound much more harmonious.

—————— ∞ ——————
Introduction

Following are 500 suggestions for making our journey through life more exciting, more fulfilling and more meaningful. Many more entries could be added to such a book, but for now 500 seemed like a good number. Some you will find funny, some sad, and some that will hit oh too close to home, but for most of us there is at least a little bit of truth in many of them.

1. More funny stories.

2. Fewer movies that are violent

3. More laughter

4. Less fear of failure

5. More flattery

6. Less fighting and arguing

7. More politeness

8. Less criticizing

9. More smiles

10. Less pimples

11. More people that care

12. Less fat and cholesterol in food

13. More understanding

14. Fewer necessary car repairs

15. More parties where we know at least two people

16. Less worry

17. More healthy people

18. Less political propaganda

19. More spiritual beliefs

20. Less complaining

21. More delicious foods that aren't bad for us

22. Less air pollution

23. More flowers

24. Less sadness

25. More time

26. Less time spent waiting in a doctor's office

27. More happy people

28. Less selfishness

29. More teachers that love to teach

30. Fewer egotists

31. More parking spaces when we're in a hurry

32. Less time spent standing in line

33. More movies that make us feel good

34. Less traffic when we're running late

35. More helpful neighbors

36. Fewer cold nights without a warm blanket

37. More sincere politicians

38. Less whining

39. More songs

40. Fewer dirty looks

41. More trees

42. Less time spent in elevators

43. More happy songs

44. Fewer sick people

45. More chocolate chip cookies

46. Fewer calories in a piece of chocolate cake

47. More caring politicians

48. Less money spent on utility bills

49. More enthusiasm

50. Less confusion

51. More hugs

52. Fewer negative comments made

53. More sunny days even when the sun isn't shining

54. Fewer feelings of insecurity

55. More decorations to celebrate, anything

56. Fewer frowns

57. More excitement

58. Less necessary police patrol

59. More phone calls made to loved ones

60. Fewer flies at picnics

61. More dances

62. Fewer ants at picnics

63. More walks in parks

64. Less hate

65. More walks anywhere

66. Fewer dictators

67. More childrens' paintings hung on refrigerators

68. Less time spent doing something we dislike

69. More time spent taking the stairs

70. Fewer conformity for the wrong reasons

71. More volunteers

72. Less tears

73. More parades

74. Less prejudice

75. More play time

76. Less junk mail

77. More swim lessons

78. Less waste

79. More respect for one another

80. Less miscommunication

81. More family gatherings

82. Fewer allergies

83. More love

84. Fewer items bought that need to be returned

85. More democracy

86. Fewer divorces

87. More singing

88. Less taxes

89. More unity

90. Less calorie counting

91. More picnics

92. Fewer traffic jams

93. More timely communication

94. Less inflation

95. More letters answered sincerely and promptly

96. Less overtime in a football game

97. More time spent with our families

98. Less dishonesty

99. More celebrations

100. Less noise pollution

101. More job security

102. Less shame

103. More convertibles

104. Less necessary court time

105. More soft cushions

106. Fewer opinionated people

107. More energy

108. Fewer flat tires

109. More sharing

110. Less deception

111. More believers

112. Less credit card fraud

113. More trips to take

114. Fewer dead batteries

115. More candlelight dinners

116. Fewer detours

117. More compassion for our fellow man

118. Fewer commercials

119. More green grass to play on

120. Less starvation

121. More dime stores where items really cost a dime

122. Less pain

123. More trunk space

124. Fewer sick days missed

125. More recycling done

126. Fewer critics

127. More days spent at the zoo

128. Less skepticism

129. More trust

130. Fewer broken promises

131. More family portraits taken

132. Less necessary ironing

133. More adventure

134. Less to worry about

135. More busy hands and busy minds

136. Less time spent feeling unloved

137. More cheering

138. Fewer insecure people

139. More appreciation for the arts

140. Fewer unhappy people

141. More love for our work

142. Less small talk

143. More faith

144. Less disrespect

145. More balanced checkbooks

146. Fewer chores to do on the weekend

147. More pure water

148. Less time spent on hold

149. More reasons to be happy

150. Less eavesdropping

151. More immediate feedback

152. Less uncertainty

153. More creativity

154. Fewer jokes that hurt someone's feelings

155. More play time

156. Fewer cruel pranks

157. More class reunions

158. Less fear of nuclear war

159. More unharmed rain forests

160. Less negative peer pressure

161. More positive memories

162. Fewer insults

163. More self-confident people

164. Fewer people threatening to sue

165. More seats in a movie theater

166. Less of a need for malpractice insurance

167. More proud people

168. Fewer don'ts

169. More love for our fellow man

170. Less rejection

171. More clear skies

172. Less aloofness

173. More pens when we need one

174. Less deprivation

175. More clocks that keep accurate time

176. Less arrogance

177. More interest in reading

178. Less bitterness

179. More sales on items that we really want

180. Less time spent sulking

181. More games where everyone wins

182. Less conceit

183. More family trees researched

184. Less betrayal

185. More honesty

186. Less indifference

187. More front page headlines that are positive

188. Less tunnel vision

189. More time spent holding hands

190. Less fear for our own safety

191. More admiration for the right reasons

192. Less blame

193. More sunsets shared

194. Less doubt

195. More causes worth believing in

196. Less spite

197. More applause

198. Less exploitation

199. More do's

200. Less famine

201. More sincerity

202. Less discrimination

203. More of our aspirations shared

204. Less guilt

205. More yes'

206. Less political mudslinging

207. More comfortable clothes

208. Fewer preservatives in food

209. More acceptance of others

210. Less dirty language spoken

211. More certainty

212. Less static electricity

213. More positive role models

214. Less inequality

215. More poetry written

216. Less filth

217. More humor

218. Less phoniness

219. More autonomy

220. Less fury

221. More walks along the beach

222. Fewer ghettos

223. More discretion

224. Less gossip

225. More clarity

226. Less disorder

227. More vacation homes for more people

228. Fewer unpleasant experiences

229. More Sunday dinners shared with loved ones

230. Fewer grudges held

231. More forgiveness

232. Fewer bones in the fish we eat

233. More efficiency

234. Less fraud

235. More altruism

236. Less grief

237. More candor

238. Fewer hurdles to cross

239. More humility

240. Fewer imitations

241. More gratitude

242. Less hypocrisy

243. More lasting friendships

244. Less illiteracy

245. More willingness to help someone in need

246. Less bigotry

247. More smiles from store clerks

248. Fewer feelings of hopelessness

249. More seconds to play that favorite video game

250. Less blackmail

251. More understanding parents

252. Less impatience

253. More bosses who really care

254. Less boredom

255. More romance in marriage

256. Fewer invasions of privacy

257. More surprises

258. Less nervousness

259. More comfortable beds

260. Less impertinence

261. More meals shared with someone

262. Less ridicule

263. More homemade bread

264. Less intimidation

265. More rainbows shared with someone

266. Less suspicion

267. More family traditions

268. Less insomnia

269. More homemade anything

270. Less laziness

271. More pleases

272. Less static cling

273. More thank you's

274. Fewer gimmicks

275. More gaiety

276. Less isolation

277. More gardens

278. Fewer experienced losses

279. More tea in the afternoon

280. Fewer interruptions

281. More respect for education

282. Fewer hurt feelings

283. More thoughtfulness

284. Less greed

285. More guarantees on what we buy

286. Less dissatisfaction

287. More initiative taken

288. Less mayhem

289. More shared umbrellas on a rainy day

290. Less slander

291. More passion

292. Less libel

293. More curiosity

294. Less meddling into other's affairs

295. More insight

296. Less struggling

297. More stories read to children

298. Fewer adversaries

299. More integrity

300. Less nagging

301. More tolerance

302. Less neglect

303. More leisure time

304. Less irritability

305. More of a desire to learn

306. Less anger

307. More affection

308. Less news that's shocking

309. More profit from our labors

310. Less destruction

311. More love songs

312. Less pessimism

313. More roses sent to loved ones

314. Less resentment

315. More green pastures

316. Less despair

317. More of a capacity to love

318. Less jealously

319. More merry-go-rounds

320. Less suffering

321. More food for hungry people

322. Less harassment

323. More patience

324. Fewer diseases without cures

325. More modesty

326. Less worry about our possessions

327. More generosity

328. Fewer phobias and reasons for them

329. More good news

330. Less yelling at our children

331. More reciprocity that makes us feel good

332. Less quarreling

333. More open-mindedness

334. Less racism

335. More nurturing

336. Less violence

337. More acceptance of responsibility for our own actions

338. Less carelessness

339. More ocean views

340. Less disappointment

341. More patriotism

342. Less rivalry

343. More cars that get better gas mileage

344. Fewer judgmental people

345. More peace

346. Fewer spankings

347. More optimism

348. Less tailgating

349. More meals served on the good dishes

350. Less shrinkage in clothing

351. More delight at what we see when we look into a mirror

352. Less terrorism

353. More visits by loved ones

354. Less sour grapes

355. More cookouts

356. Less drudgery

357. More scientists discovering cures

358. Less fatigue

359. More positive notes written by teachers

360. Less tension

361. More tranquillity

362. Less anxiety

363. More pristine land

364. Less toxic waste

365. More cool summer breezes shared with loved ones

366. Less fear

367. More moral support from others

368. Less turmoil

369. More notes written to loved ones just to say "I love you"

370. Fewer sore throats

371. More praise

372. Fewer tragedies

373. More homemade soup

374. Fewer stomach ulcers

375. More spontaneity

376. Fewer people having ulterior motives

377. More space

378. Less commotion

379. More time spent doing nothing and enjoying it

380. Less rebellion

381. More serenades

382. Less ambiguity

383. More rejoicing

384. Less unemployment

385. More PS's added to letters that brighten someone's day

386. Less uneasiness

387. More courtesy

388. Less secrecy

389. More welcome mats

390. Less vengeance

391. More tact

392. Less dejection

393. More street trolleys

394. Less absenteeism

395. More team players

396. Fewer distractions

397. More flexibility

398. Fewer potholes in the road

399. More unconditional love

400. Less poverty

401. More loyalty

402. Less apathy

403. More timely answers

404. Less alienation

405. More courage

406. Fewer backaches

407. More sensitivity

408. Fewer crank calls

409. More promises that are kept

410. Less loneliness

411. More favors done for one another

412. Fewer cavities

413. More dedication

414. Less embarrassment

415. More hope

416. Fewer dilemmas to deal with

417. More time spent just talking to our children

418. Less discouragement

419. More determination

420. Less emphasis placed on the negative

421. More games played

422. Fewer dead ends

423. More winter vacations

424. Less weariness

425. More expectations that are met

426. Less fear of war

427. More international peace

428. Less hostility

429. More crackling fires in winter shared with someone

430. Less desperation

431. More empathy for one another

432. Fewer front page headlines that are depressing

433. More afternoon naps

434. Less suspicion

435. More of a desire to learn

436. Less denial

437. More friends

438. Less depreciation on the cars that we buy

439. More visits to amusement parks

440. Less worry about the economy

441. More bubble baths

442. Fewer engagements broken

443. More bird feeders hung in yards

444. Less confusing directions

445. More marriages that last

446. Fewer misleading advertisements

447. More imagination

448. Fewer leaky faucets

449. More train rides

450. Fewer hardships

451. More idealism

452. Less darkness

453. More stories shared over a campfire

454. Fewer obstacles, real or imagined, that we see in our way

455. More silk sheets

456. Fewer no's

457. More of the exact change when we need it

458. Fewer fallacies

459. More choices

460. Less time spent feeling inadequate

461. More classic movies

462. Less frustration

463. More guilt free desserts

464. Less time spent worrying about our past mistakes

465. More cheer

466. Fewer inconsiderate people

467. More value for the dollar

468. Fewer relapses after an illness

469. More private diaries that are kept private

470. Less indigestion

471. More cooperation

472. Fewer monotonous chores that need doing

473. More encouragement

474. Fewer incomplete answers to our questions

475. More self-esteem

476. Fewer quitters

477. More cohesion in relationships

478. Fewer insincere people

479. More eye contact when speaking to another person

480. Less indifference toward others

481. More equality

482. Less shoddy craftsmanship

483. More flaky piecrusts

484. Fewer temper tantrums when we don't get our own way

485. More clean air to breathe

486. Fewer neglected children

487. More jobs for those wishing to work

488. Less insidiousness

489. More ingenuity

490. Fewer unsociable people

491. More sound investments made

492. Less inoperable cancers

493. More maple syrup served with pancakes

494. Less regret

495. More honor

496. Fewer people in the helping profession that don't enjoy helping

497. More scenic drives taken

498. Less dust

499. More gifts given without expecting one in return

500. Less paperwork

Epilogue

With more to do and less to do it looks like we had better get busy doing.

About the Author

My goal in writing is to show how powerful words can be. They bring out the best in us, or unfortunately, they can bring out the worst. I prefer bringing out the best.